# By Special Arrangement

## BEAUTIFUL CHORAL ARRANGEMENTS
## OF FAVOURITE CLASSICS

### SELECTED AND EDITED BY RALPH ALLWOOD

The Novello Choral Programme

NOV072523
ISBN 978-0-85360-988-8

Cover illustration: Jan Davidsz de Heem,
*Flowers in a glass vase on a stone ledge* c. 1660.
Reproduction by permission of the Syndics of the
Fitzwilliam Museum, Cambridge.
Cover design by Miranda Harvey.

Printed in the EU.

*By Special Arrangement*, sung by the Rodolfus Choir,
directed by Ralph Allwood and Ben Parry,
is available on Herald A V Publications (HAVPCD 242).

# CONTENTS

# INTRODUCTION

Four or five years ago the Rodolfus Choir performed Clytus Gottwald's arrangement of Mahler's orchestral song *Ich bin der Welt abhanden gekommen*. The experience of singing such powerful music, normally the preserve of a large romantic orchestra, was overwhelming. I began wondering whether it would be possible to repeat the experience with other music, particularly by composers whose work would normally be denied to choral singers. For a long time, Tchaikovsky's First String Quartet has been a special favourite of mine (Tolstoy was once reduced to tears by a performance of this piece). Samuel Barber, of course, had decided that choirs should have the chance to perform his emotionally charged *Adagio for Strings*. I let it be known that I intended to produce a CD of arrangements of such excellent non-choral music. Before long, several friends had come up with inspired ideas, and we set about arranging and performing, adjusting and perfecting.

Two of these arrangements are the result of sudden discoveries. Robert Quinney realised that, by happy coincidence, the words of Wordsworth's *Ode To The Cuckoo* precisely fitted – to the note – Delius' *On Hearing The First Cuckoo In Spring*, and Leo Hussain noticed that Elizabeth Barrett Browning's *How Do I Love Thee?* easily matched Chopin's *Etude in E Major*. Finding the right text was the greatest difficulty in our project, but only once, in Tchaikovsky's *Danse De La Fée Dragée* from *The Nutcracker*, did we resort to nonsense words. Often, well-known religious texts fitted the bill, as with Chopin's Prelude in C minor and Bach's famous Air 'on the G String' – I couldn't resist including Jonathan Rathbone's arrangement, with its mischievous 'blue-note' additions. Puccini's *Crisantemi* (*Chrysanthemums*), originally written for string quartet and arranged by him for string orchestra, proved a much more difficult nut to crack. Though an ideal candidate for choral arrangement, it was several years before I mentioned the problem to Lora Sansun. She came up with the ingenious idea of using some Italian words from a cycle of sacred madrigals by Domenico Mazzocchi, describing the anguish of the Virgin Mary on losing her young son in the temple.

Most of the pieces in this collection are arrangements of music for orchestral groups or for keyboard. Of the three songs, the two by Schubert preserve the original accompaniment: the tortuous chromatic harmonies of his nostalgic *Litany for the Feast of All Souls* are enhanced by legato vocal lines, and the great *An Die Musik* is a fitting partner.

I have performed the works in this collection many times, and I hope this publication will bring you as much enjoyment.

RALPH ALLWOOD  *Eton College, March 2000*

# AGNUS DEI
## ADAGIO FOR STRINGS OP.11

*Words from the Ordinary of the Mass*      Samuel Barber      *Transcribed by the composer*

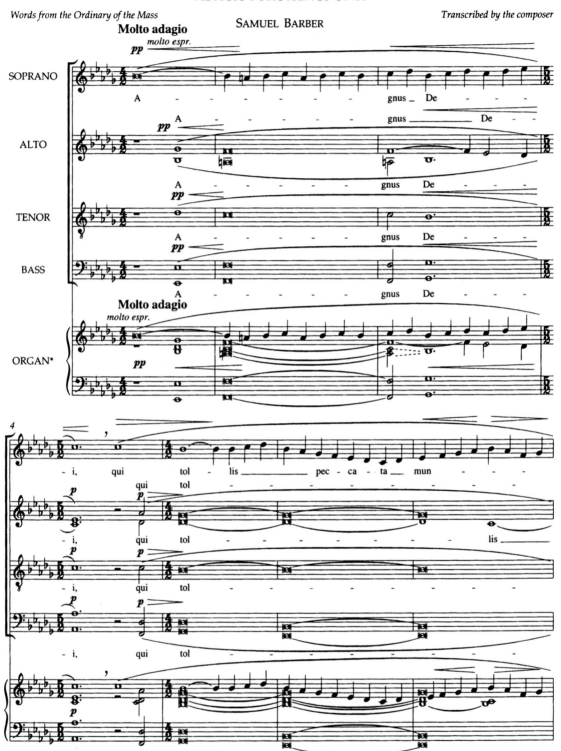

* If the chorus is large and expert enough, may be sung *a cappella*.
Note: The various individual singers on each part should breathe at different places, especially in the long phrases and held notes,
in order to achieve a more sustained quality.

begin to add on the organ, use 8' Pedals only until bar 35 (♩)

# AN DIE MUSIK

## ADAPTED FROM THE SOLO SONG D.547

Franz Schubert

Words by Franz von Schober

Arranged by Lydia Smallwood

# AVE VERUM CORPUS

## ADAPTED FROM THE MOTET K.618

WOLFGANG AMADEUS MOZART

*Chant in honour of the Blessed Sacrament*

*Arranged by Ben Parry*

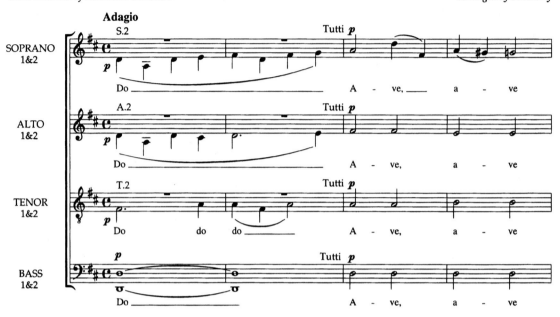

# AVE MARIA
## STRING QUARTET NO. 1 IN D

PIOTR ILYICH TCHAIKOVSKY

*Antiphon to the Blessed Virgin Mary*

*Arranged by Ralph Allwood & Edward Gardner*

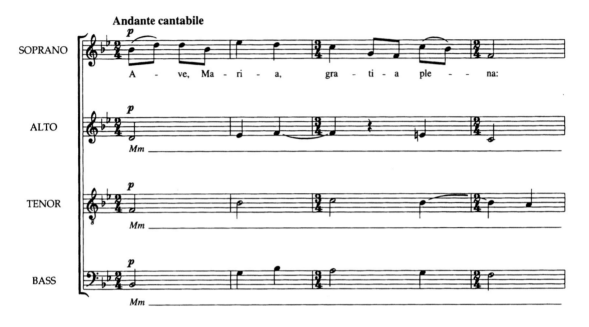

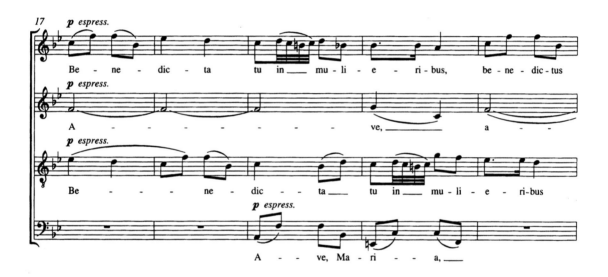

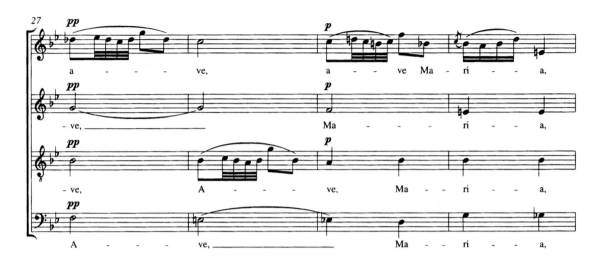

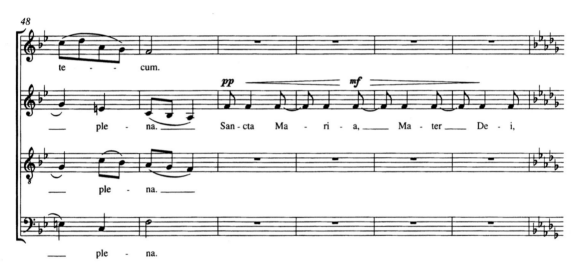

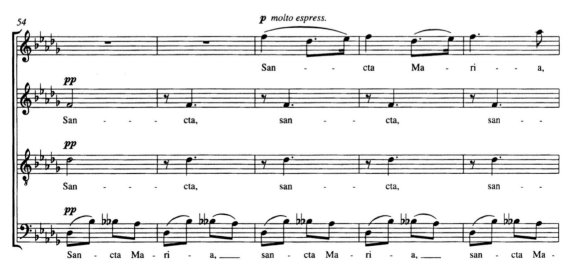

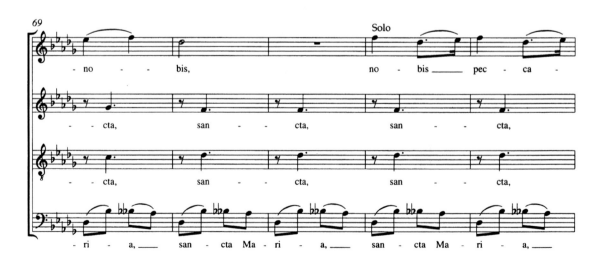

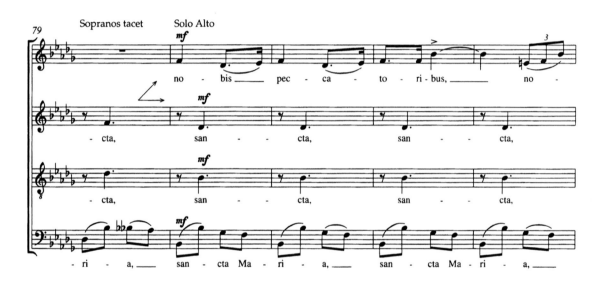

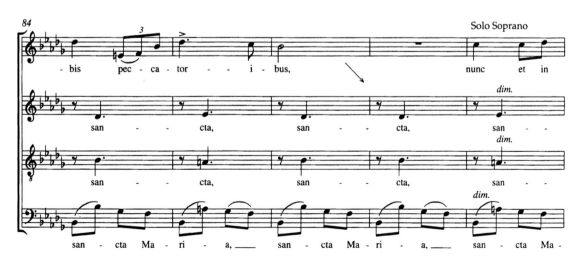

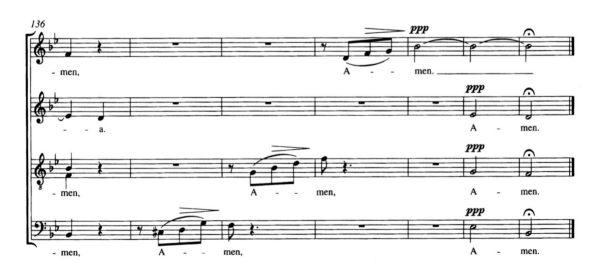

# CHRISTO SMARRITO
## (The Lost Christ)
### STRING QUARTET MOVEMENT 'CRISANTEMI'

GIACOMO PUCCINI

*Text extracts from sacred madrigals*
*by Domenico Mazzocchi*

Arranged by Ralph Allwood & Lora Sansun

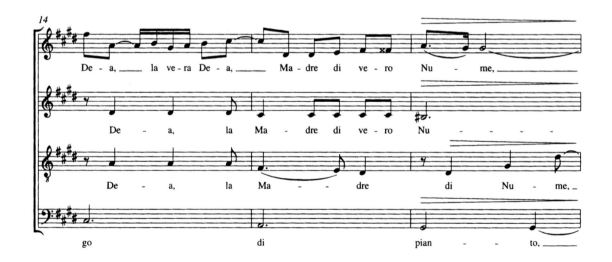

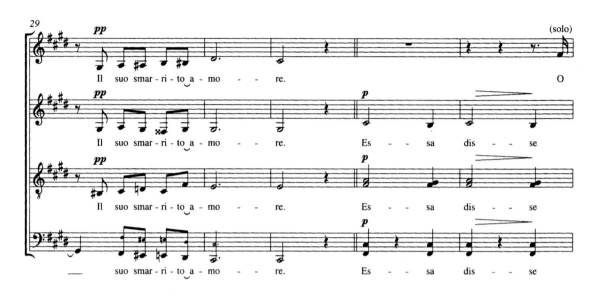

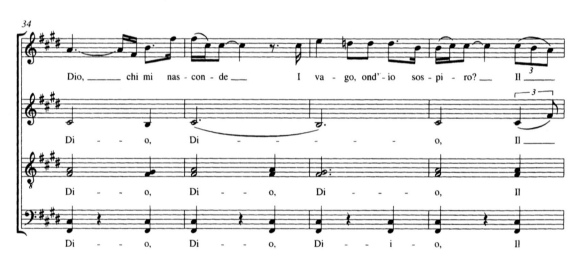

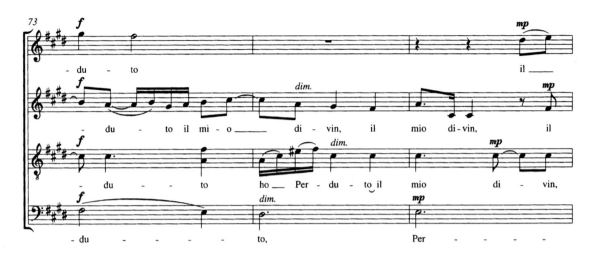

# DANSE DE LA FÉE-DRAGÉE

## FROM THE NUTCRACKER

Piotr Ilyich Tchaikovsky

*Nonsense words by Lydia Smallwood*

*Arranged by Leo Hussain & Ralph Allwood*

*Pronounce 'plum' as 'pl'm', to imitate a pizzicato double bass.

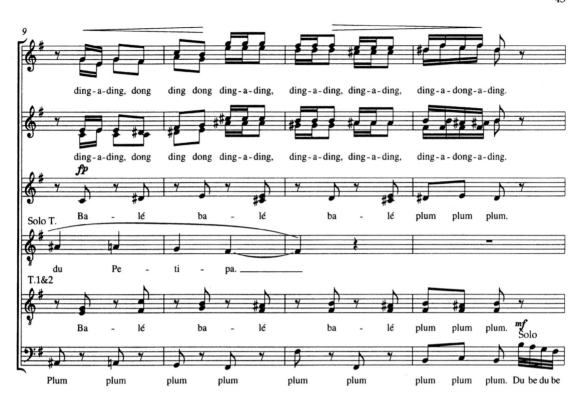

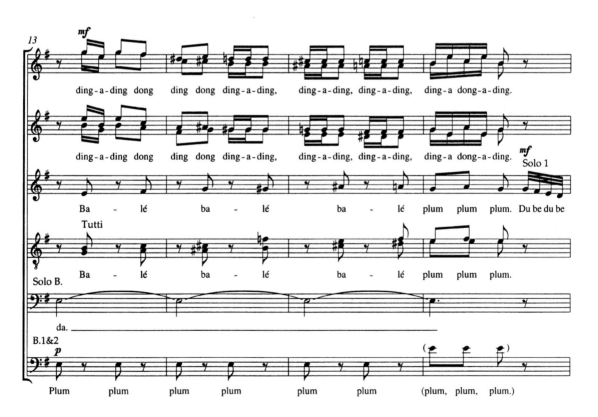

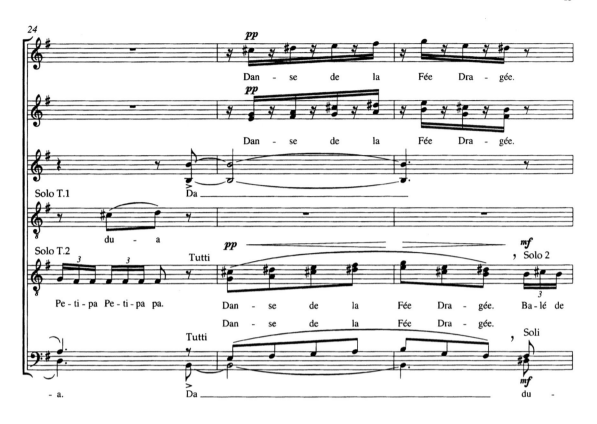

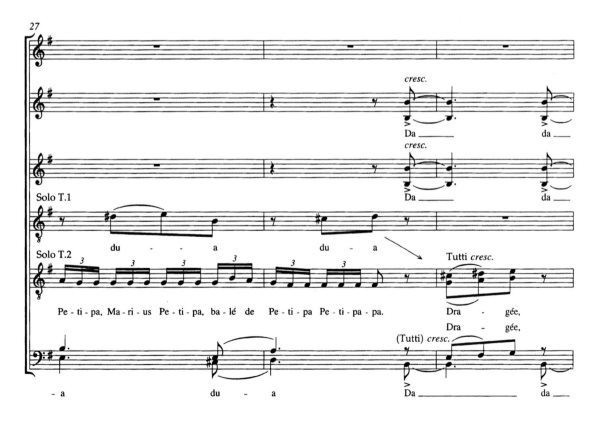

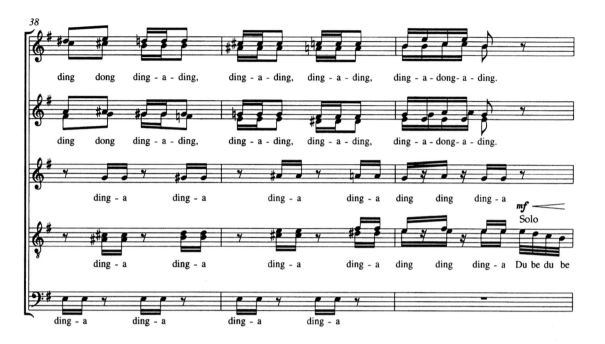

# DIE MIT TRÄNEN

## PRELUDE IN Bb MINOR
### from Book 1 of The Well-tempered Clavier

JOHANN SEBASTIAN BACH

*Text from Psalm 126, v.6*

*Arranged by Ralph Allwood & Lora Sansun*

# HOW DO I LOVE THEE?

### AFTER ÉTUDE IN E MAJOR, OP.10 NO.3

FRYDERYK CHOPIN

*Poem by Elizabeth Barrett Browning*

*Arranged by Leo Hussain*
*For two choirs*

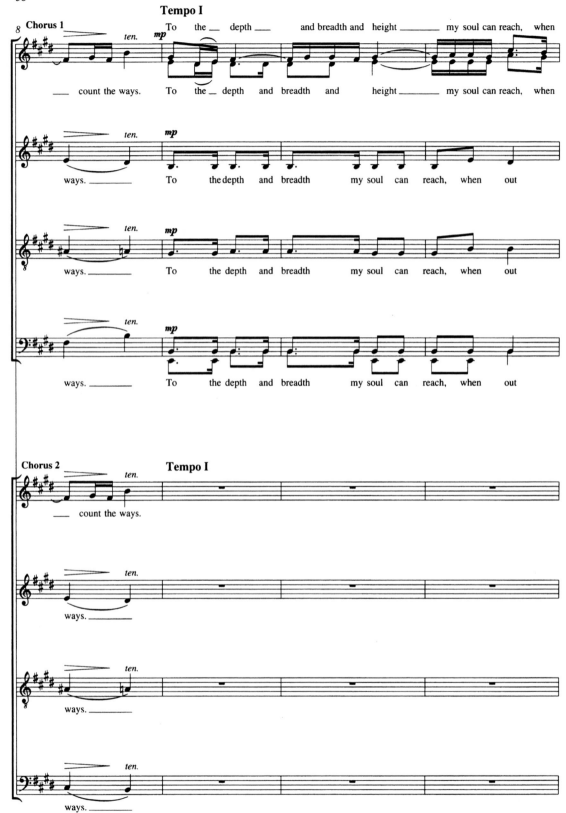

58

# LITANEI (auf das Fest aller Seelen)

### ADAPTED FROM THE SOLO SONG D.343

FRANZ SCHUBERT

Words by Johann Georg Jacobi

Arranged by Ralph Allwood

Al - le See - len ruh'n _____ in Frie - den!

Al - le See - len ruh'n _____ in Frie - den!

Al - le See - len ruh'n _____ in Frie - den!

Al - le See - len ruh'n _____ in Frie - den!

*pp*        *cresc.*

# ON HEARING THE
# FIRST CUCKOO IN SPRING

## ORCHESTRAL TONE POEM

FREDERICK DELIUS

*Poem 'To The Cuckoo' by William Wordsworth*

*Arranged by Robert Quinney*

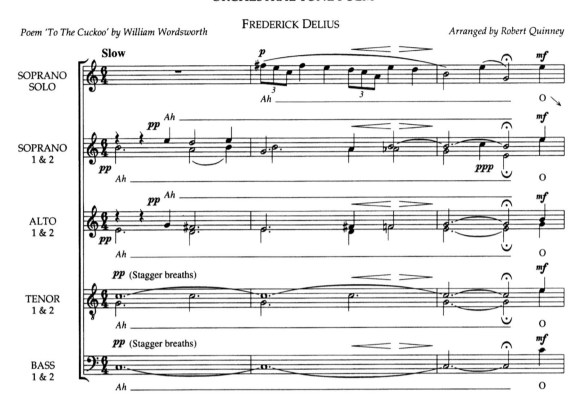

* Bar 20: if the bass part is too low, sing up an octave, and transfer B.1 part to tenors (also up an octave).

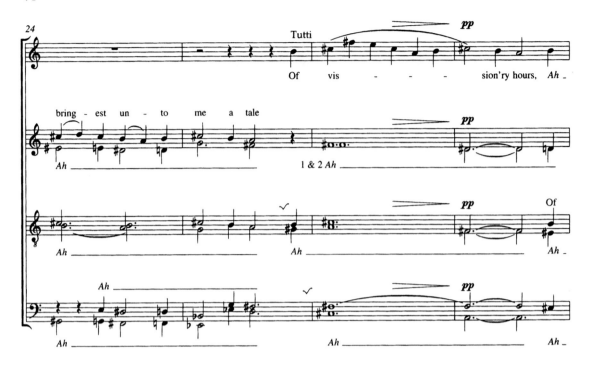

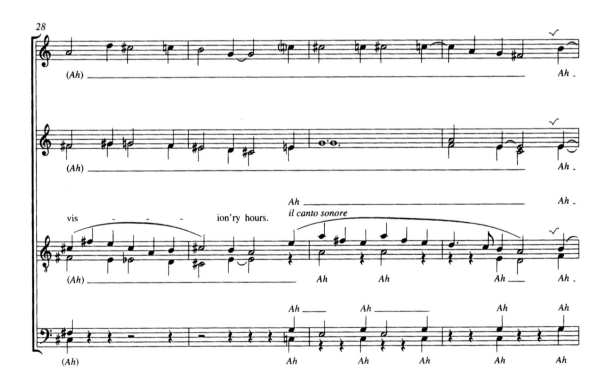

* T.1 bar 33: if this is too much, join the 2nd Tenors and let the Altos do it.

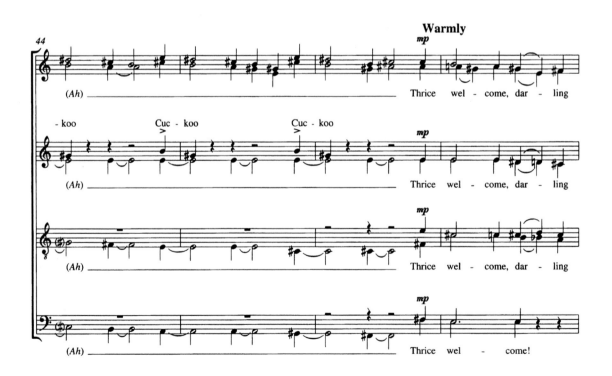

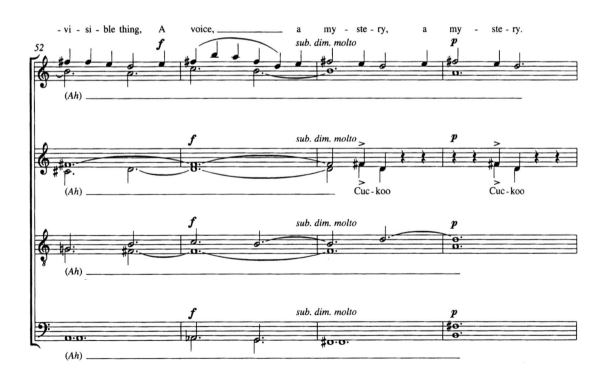

Semi-chorus, perhaps 2 voices per part

**Rather broader**

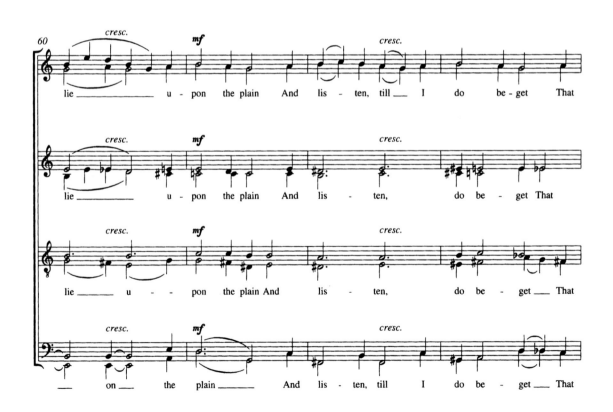

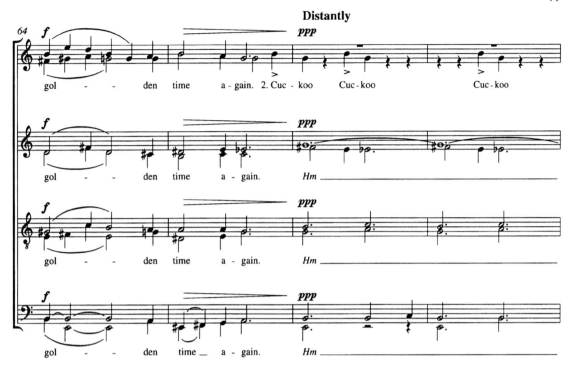

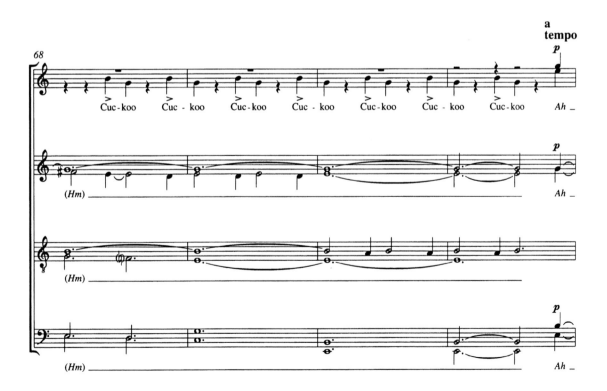

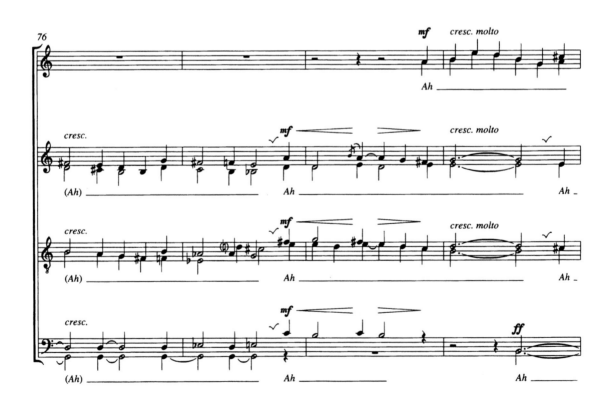

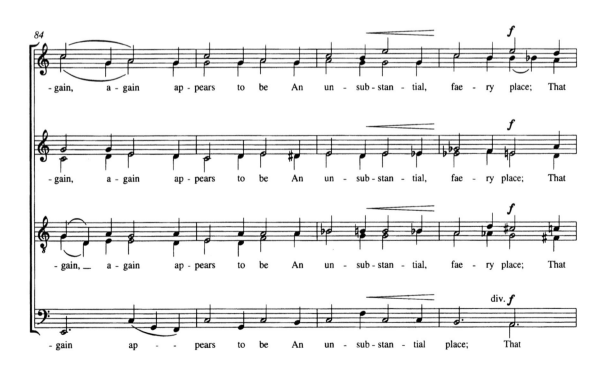

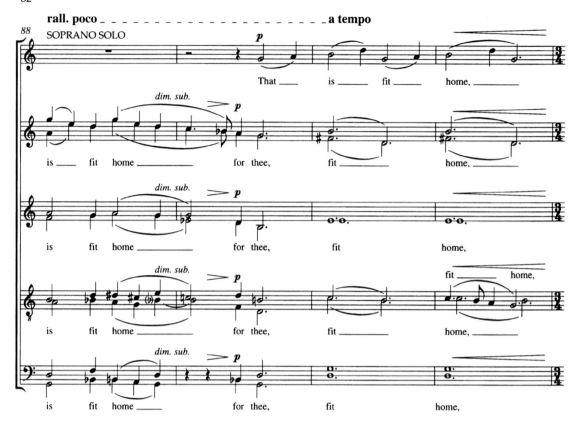

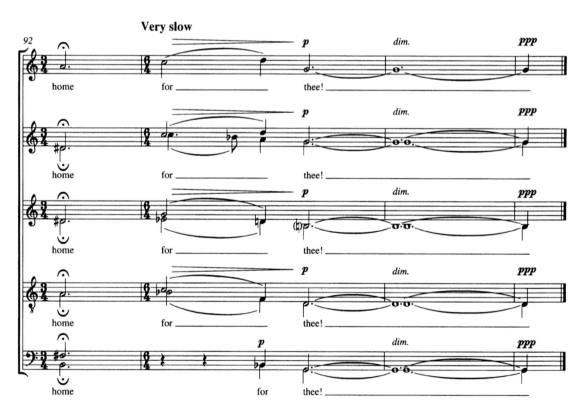

# REQUIEM AETERNAM

## AIR ON THE G STRING FROM SUITE NO. 3 IN D

### JOHANN SEBASTIAN BACH

*Words from the Requiem Mass*

*Arranged by Jonathan Rathbone*

\* Alto 2 bars 1-12 could be sung with/by Tenor 1 if preferred.

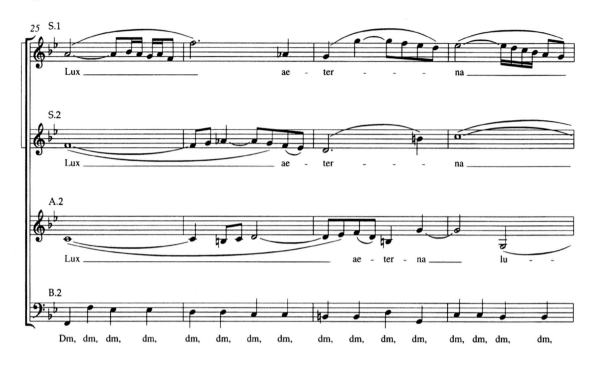

# PRO PECCATIS SUAE GENTIS

## PRELUDE IN C MINOR FROM 24 PRELUDES OP.28

### FRYDERYK CHOPIN

*Words from 'Stabat Mater' ascribed to Giacopone da Todi*

*Arranged by Ralph Allwood*

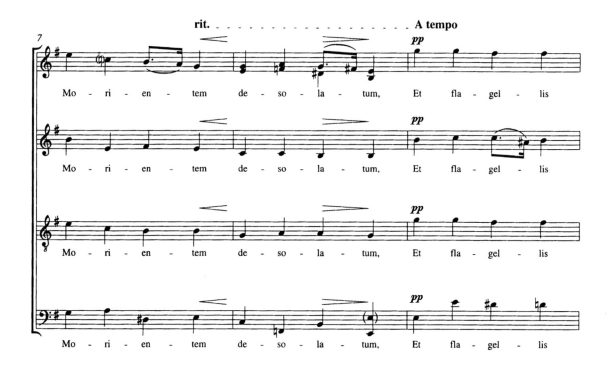

# SOLVEIGS SANG

## SOLVEIG'S SONG FROM PEER GYNT OP.23 NO.9

EDVARD GRIEG

Text by Henrik Ibsen
English text by Lora Sansun

Arranged by Alexander Milner & Lora Sansun

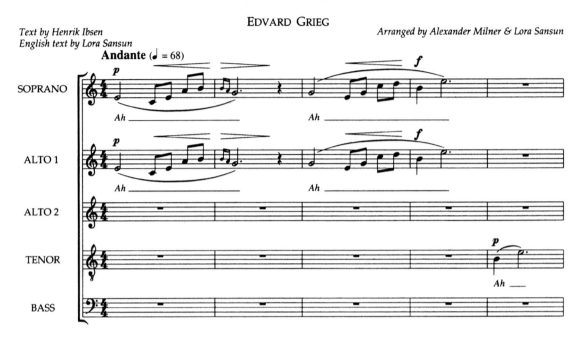

96

**Allegretto con moto**

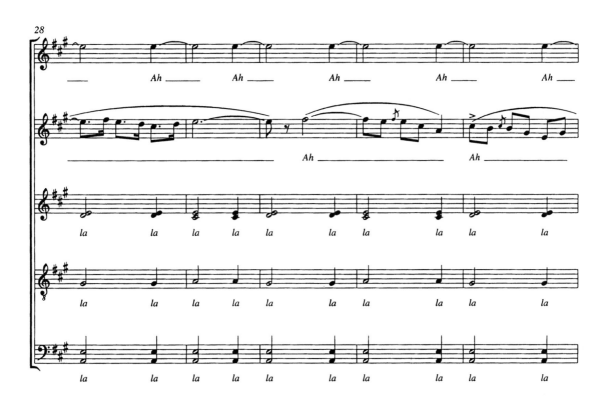

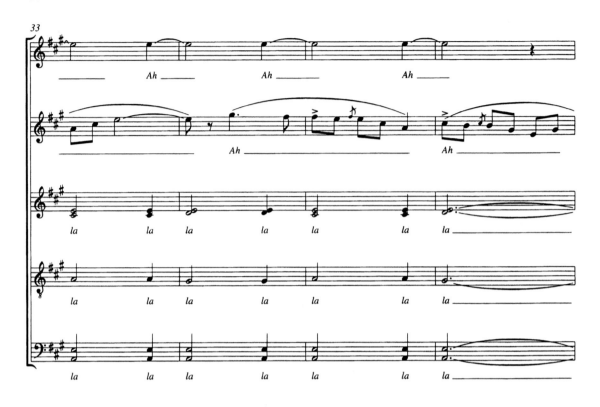

**Tempo I**

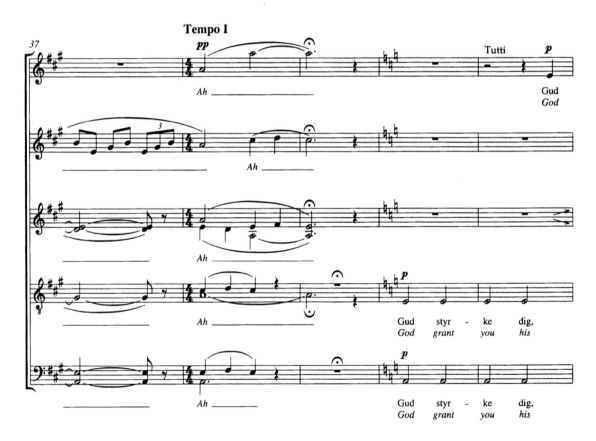

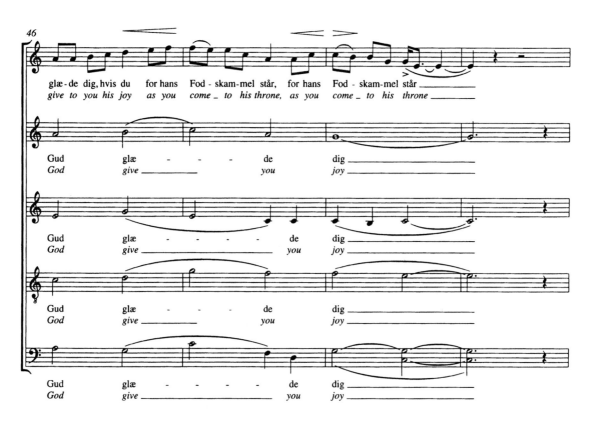

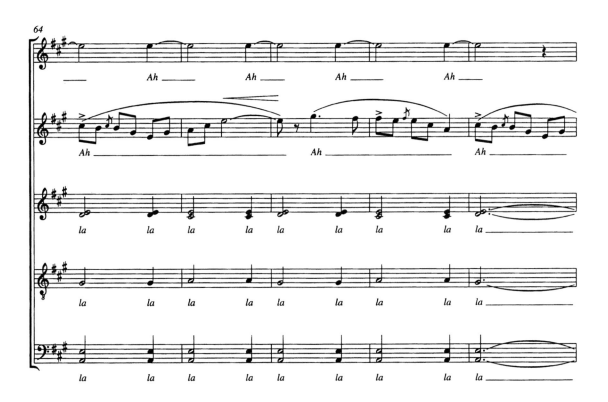

**Tempo I**

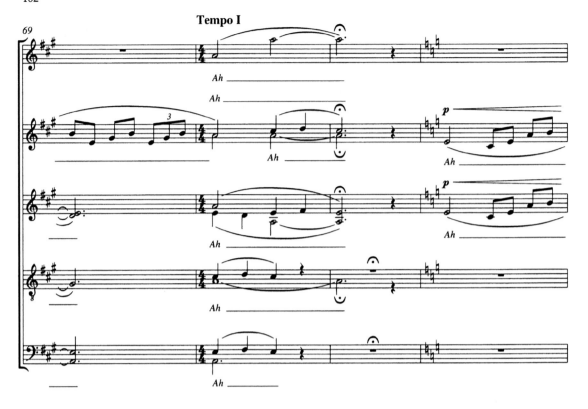

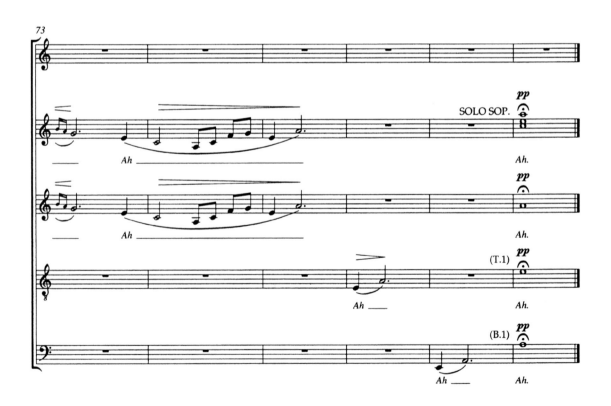

# Pronunciation guide for SOLVEIGS SANG

by Lora Sansun

Text by Henrik Ibsen from *Peer Gynt*

*(letters in brackets indicate the sound of the previous vowel as if you were going to
say the whole word)*

Kanskje vil der gå både Vinter og Vår,

*Kun-sheh vill dair go(t) bo-de Vin-terr o vorr,*
             *(o sounds are as in "stop" i.e. no diphthong*
                 *r is rolled)*

Og neste Sommer med og det hele År

*O neç-te çommmer mè(r) o de héé-le or*
             *(ç as in French usage or like the English ss – as in "less")*

Men engang vil du komme, det vet jeg vist,

*Men ain-gang vill dü kommm-er, de vertt yay viçt*
                 *(viçt like English "mist")*

Og jeg skal nok vente, for det lovte jeg sidst.

*O yay skulll nokk venn-te ffor de lo(r)ff-te yay çiçt*
                 *(skal is half-way between skall and skull*
                 *lovte has the o like the English "saw"*
                 *and ff is like the English "four")*

Gud styrke dig, hvor du I Verden går,

*Güd stürrr-ke day vor dü ee vver-denn gore*
                 *(roll the r lots in stürrrke & emphasise double v)*

Gud glæde dig, hvis du for hans Fodskammel står

*Güd gleerde day viç dü ffor hanç ffor-skammmell stor*
                 *(ffot as in English "hot")*

Her skal jeg vente til du kommer igjen;

*Haar skull yay venn-te till dü kommm-err ee-yen*

Og venter du hist oppe, vi træffes der, min Ven!

*O venn-ter dü hiçt oppp-pe vee trèffeç daar min venn*
                 *(the p in oppe nearly stops the sound*
                 *& min like the English "tin")*

It is not possible to capture the lovely subtleties of the sound of Norwegian in this attempt to
guide the pronunciation. Do seek out the real thing and get a native's version of it.

# Translations of song texts

**Agnus Dei** (p.6)
Lamb of God, who takest away the sins of the world: have mercy upon us.
Lamb of God, who takest away the sins of the world: grant us peace.

**An Die Musik** (p.16)
O sacred art, in how many gloomy hours, when Life's mad whirl constrained me, have you inflamed my heart into a warmer love, have you carried me into a better world! Often has a sigh from your harp escaped, a sweet, holy chord from you has given me a glimpse of better times from Heaven; you sacred art, I thank you for this.

**Ave Maria** (p.24)
Hail Mary, full of grace, the Lord is with thee. Blessed art thou among women and blessed is the fruit of thy womb, Jesus. Holy Mary, Mother of God, pray for us sinners, now and at the hour of our death. Amen.

**Ave Verum Corpus** (p.20)
Hail, true Body born of the Virgin Mary, the same who suffered on the Cross for man. Thou, whose side was pierced and flowed with water and blood, suffer us to taste of thee in the trial of death.

**Christo Smarrito** (p.33)
Text extracts taken from a cycle of sacred madrigals by Domenico Mazzocchi (1592-1665)
(*The Lost Christ*)
She sighed, shedding
A wide river of tears,
The true goddess,
Mother of the true divinity,
Searching for her heart,
Her lost and fugitive love.

(She said)
O Lord, who hides from me
Him for whom I sigh?
I call him, and he does not respond,
I search and cannot find him.

Alas, my heart is torn
Between suspicion and hope,
My spirit flees from me,
Fled is all that I love,
Vanished is my joy,
I have lost, alas, my divine boy.

Guard over him O Almighty Father,
Thou the eternal defender.

**Die Mit Tränen** (p.49)
Those who sow in tears shall reap in joy.

**Litanei** (p.68)
Rest in peace all souls, those who have finished with anxious torment, who have ended sweet dreams, who, fed up with life and hardly born, have departed from this world: all souls rest in peace! Maiden souls, full of love, whose tears are endless, who have left a false friend and disowned a blind world: all who have departed from here, all souls rest in peace! And those who never laughed at the sun, who were wakeful on the thorns under the moon, to see God's face in the pure light of Heaven: all who have departed from here, all souls rest in peace!

**Pro Peccatis Suae Gentis** (p.92)
She saw Jesus suffering for the sins of his own people; she saw her own sweet Son forsaken in death, and subjected to the scourge; then he gave up the ghost.

**Requiem Aeternam** (p.83)
Eternal rest grant them, O Lord, and let perpetual light shine upon them. May light eternal shine upon them, O Lord, with thy Saints for ever; for thou art merciful.

Printed in the United Kingdom
by Lightning Source UK Ltd.
123906UK00001B/71-156/A